A Day in

An illustrated story written in the C programming language

By Shari Eskenas
Illustrated by Ana Quintero Villafraz

Published by Sundae Electronics LLC
https://www.sundaelectronics.com

First edition 2020.

ISBN 978-1-7359079-0-1 (Hardcover)
ISBN 978-1-7359079-1-8 (Paperback)
ISBN 978-1-7359079-2-5 (eBook)

Logic is all around you.

Look for it. – S.E.

Once upon a time, there were two kids (a brother and sister) who loved computers. One day they did so many fun activities and had such an epic day that they wanted to share the story of that day with computers. They began by telling the story to some laptop computers.

But the computers couldn't understand them! Computers read and understand information in their own language- a computer programming language!

The kids needed to write **code** to communicate with the computers. Code is a set of instructions written for a computer to perform tasks. Similarly, a recipe like the one below is a set of instructions to perform the task of making a chocolate cake!

A **program** is a collection of code that can be run by a computer. Before the kids could write programs, they had to choose a programming language to write them in. There were so many to choose from!

As they were thinking about what language to choose, they went to a bakery and bought donuts. When they got home, they saw an oddly shaped donut in the box that looked like the letter C.

This reminded the kids of the C language. They did some research and learned that C is a widely used language that has influenced the code of other popular programming languages. This led them to choose the C language for their first programs.

The kids found that there are rules for writing code, called the **syntax**. For example, in the C language they must put a semicolon at the end of each **statement** (a complete program instruction). To remember this, they drew semicolons all around the house.

The kids started off by writing their first program:

```c
//Before the day began

#include <stdio.h>

int main(void)
{
    printf("We can't wait for tomorrow!");

    return 0;
}
```

This is what they learned:

`//Before the day began` is a **comment**. A comment is a note you write for a person reading the program- it's ignored by the computer! A comment on a single line is made with a double forward slash // in front of the words.

`main()` is a **function**. A function is a block of code (within curly braces) that contains instructions. Every C program needs a `main()` function, where the program begins running.

`printf()` is a function in the **C standard library** that **outputs** text to the computer screen. A **library** is a collection of functions and data that can be used in your code. The C standard library is built into the C language.

`stdio.h` is a **header file** that contains information needed for the C standard library's **input** and **output** functions to work. This header file is needed to use the `printf()` function. It is included in the program with `#include`.

`return 0` returns a value of `0` to the system running the program, which is typically used as a signal that the program successfully finished. The `int` before `main()` indicates the return value is an **integer** (a whole number that doesn't have a decimal point). The `void` indicates that the `main()` function does not receive any data.

When the program above is run (executed), the sentence `We can't wait for tomorrow!` is printed on the computer screen.

After spending more time studying the C language, the kids were ready to tell the story of their epic day. In this book, you'll see the programs that were given to the computers. There are directions at the end of the book for running the programs on YOUR computer! I hope you enjoy the story as much as the computers did!

We were so excited for the day ahead, we couldn't sleep. At midnight, we each counted 5 unicorns before finally drifting into a deep slumber.

```c
//Fall asleep program

#include <stdio.h>

int main(void)
{
    int unicorns = 0; //variable declaration

    //Count 5 unicorns with a for loop
    for (int count = 0; count < 5; count++)
    {
        unicorns = unicorns + 1;
    }

    printf("I counted %d unicorns and fell asleep", unicorns);

    return 0;
}
```

unicorns **is called a variable. It stores the number of unicorns counted:**
A **variable** stores a value in the computer's memory and the programmer gives it a name. Before variables are used, they must be declared with a **data type** such as int for storing an integer. Variables can be assigned a starting value (initialized) when they are declared.

A for **loop repeats a block of code (in curly braces { }) for a given number of times:**
In this program, the loop repeats 5 times to count 5 unicorns. In the loop's header, for (int count = 0; count < 5; count++), int count = 0 declares count as an integer and initializes it to 0. Next, this process is followed:

Step 1. The condition count < 5 is tested for being true or false.
Step 2. If the condition is true, the for loop's code block is executed. If it's false, the code block is not executed and the program continues by jumping to the line of code after the for loop.
Step 3. After the code block executes, count++ increases count by 1 with the **increment operator ++**.

Steps 1 through 3 are repeated until the condition count < 5 is false (when count = 5). The program then proceeds to the printf() statement.

This is how unicorns **becomes 5:**
The statement in the code block unicorns = unicorns + 1 increases the value of unicorns by 1. Since unicorns was initialized to 0 and the for loop repeats 5 times, unicorns = 5 when the for loop ends.

The printf() **function prints** I counted 5 unicorns and fell asleep **on the screen:**
When printf() outputs text to the screen, %d is replaced by the value of unicorns, which is now 5. %d is called a **format specifier** for an int data type.

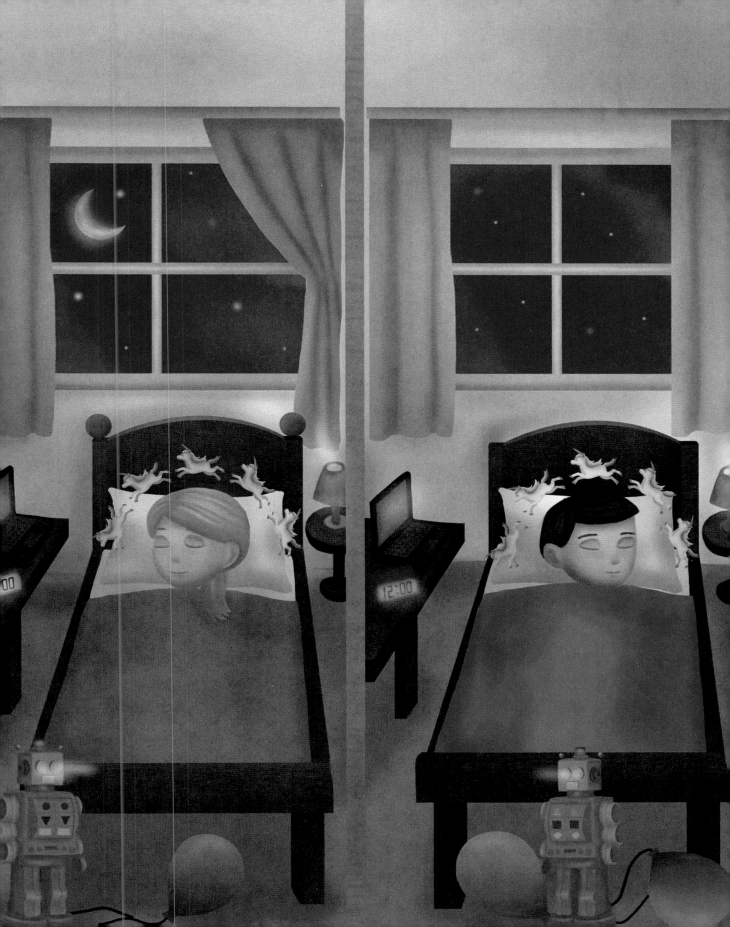

If the time is 9 AM, the alarm will turn on and we'll wake up. If it's not 9 AM, we'll be sleeping and the alarm will be off. It's 9 AM, so the alarm turned on. We're jumping out of bed!

```c
//Wake up program

#include <stdio.h>

#define OFF 0
#define ON 1
#define AM 0
#define PM 1

int main(void)
{
        int clock_time = 9, time_of_day = 0, alarm;

        if (clock_time == 9 && time_of_day == AM)
        {
                alarm = ON;
                printf("It's 9 AM, wake up! Jump out of bed!");
        }
        else
        {
                alarm = OFF;
                printf("Sweet dreams…");
        }

        return 0;
}
```

The if…else statement tests if a condition is true or false:
If the **expression** in parentheses is true, the if code block is executed. If it's false, the else code block is executed. In the if expression in this program, the double equal sign == tests for "equals to" and && means **logical AND**. The expression tests if clock_time is equal to 9 **AND** time_of_day is equal to AM. Since the expression is true, the if code block is executed and alarm is assigned the value of ON. The printf() function prints It's 9 AM, wake up! Jump out of bed! on the screen.

The #define directive allows a constant value to be represented by a name:
OFF is defined as 0, ON is defined as 1, AM is defined as 0, and PM is defined as 1. There is no semicolon at the end of a #define statement. By defining a constant value with a meaningful name, the code is easier to read and you can change the constant's value in a single place. The name in #define is called a **macro**. It's common to use uppercase names for macros to easily distinguish them from variables. The variable time_of_day was initialized to 0, and AM means 0, so time_of_day == AM is true.

Variables of the same data type can be declared on the same line:
clock_time, time_of_day, and alarm are all declared with the int data type. The variable clock_time is initialized to 9, time_of_day is initialized to 0, and alarm is not initialized.

10

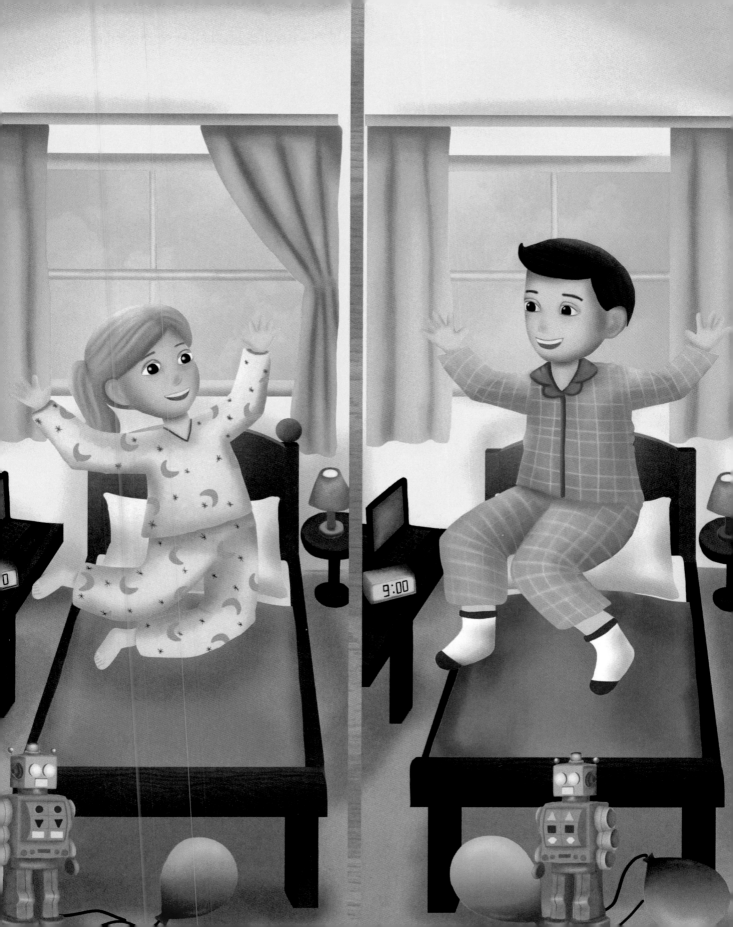

We're making 20 pancakes for breakfast. Each pancake takes 4 minutes to cook, so they will all be done in 80 minutes.

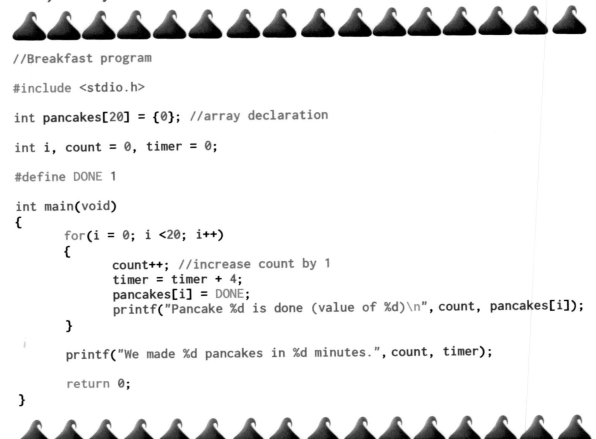

```
//Breakfast program

#include <stdio.h>

int pancakes[20] = {0}; //array declaration

int i, count = 0, timer = 0;

#define DONE 1

int main(void)
{
        for(i = 0; i <20; i++)
        {
                count++; //increase count by 1
                timer = timer + 4;
                pancakes[i] = DONE;
                printf("Pancake %d is done (value of %d)\n", count, pancakes[i]);
        }

        printf("We made %d pancakes in %d minutes.", count, timer);

        return 0;
}
```

An array stores a collection of variables (called elements) of the same data type:
The pancakes array is declared to have 20 elements of the int data type, which are all initialized to 0.

In the for loop code block:
The increment operator ++ increases the count value by 1. The timer variable's value is increased by 4. The variable i is used to access each element of the pancakes array. The first array element is pancakes[0], since the first element of an array always starts at an index of 0. The first time through the for loop, i = 0, so pancakes[0] is assigned the value of DONE, which is 1. The printf() function prints Pancake 1 is done (value of 1). The \n in printf() is a **newline** character that ends the line so that the next printf() will start printing at the beginning of the next line.

The for loop is executed 20 times:
The first loop starts at i = 0 and the last loop executes when i = 19. There are 20 array elements from pancakes[0] to pancakes[19]. The last time through the for loop, the timer value is increased to 80, pancakes[19] is assigned a value of DONE, and Pancake 20 is done (value of 1) is printed. After the for loop ends, the printf() function prints We made 20 pancakes in 80 minutes. on the screen.

We're at the beach! If the bag of chips is open or the box of cupcakes is open, and if we're playing, seagulls will be eating. If the bag of chips is open or the box of cupcakes is open, and we're not playing, we'll watch out for seagulls. Otherwise, if the bags of chips is closed and the box of cupcakes is closed, seagulls will not be eating. Since the cupcake box is open and we're playing, seagulls are eating.

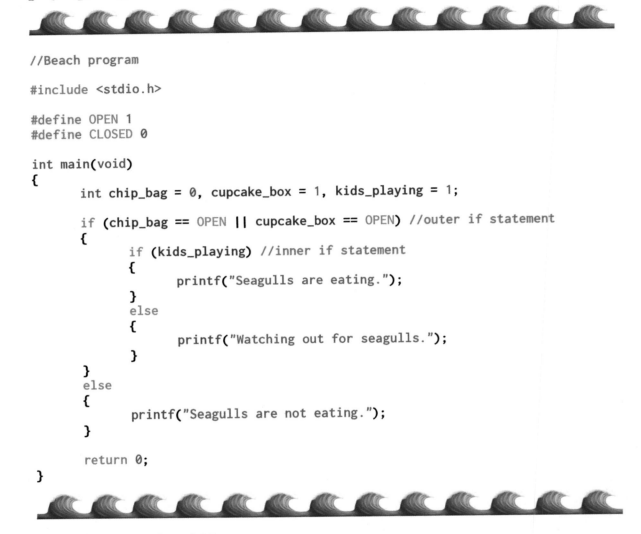

```
//Beach program

#include <stdio.h>

#define OPEN 1
#define CLOSED 0

int main(void)
{
        int chip_bag = 0, cupcake_box = 1, kids_playing = 1;

        if (chip_bag == OPEN || cupcake_box == OPEN) //outer if statement
        {
                if (kids_playing) //inner if statement
                {
                        printf("Seagulls are eating.");
                }
                else
                {
                        printf("Watching out for seagulls.");
                }
        }
        else
        {
                printf("Seagulls are not eating.");
        }

        return 0;
}
```

The symbol || means logical OR:
Therefore, the outer if expression means: if chip_bag is equal to OPEN OR if cupcake_box is equal to OPEN. Since cupcake_box has a value of 1 (and OPEN means 1), the outer if expression is true and the inner if...else statement is executed.

The inner if...else statement within the outer if code block is called a nested if...else statement:
The nested if...else statement tests if kids_playing is true. Any expression that evaluates to a non-zero value is true. Since kids_playing has a value of 1, the if condition is true and the printf() function prints Seagulls are eating. on the screen.

We're playing a carnival game! If you knock down 1 or more bottles and less than 3, you win a small unicorn. If you knock down 3 or more bottles and less than or equal to 5, you win a medium unicorn. If you knock down all 6 bottles, you win a large unicorn. Otherwise, try again. We each knocked down all 6 bottles, so we each won a large unicorn!

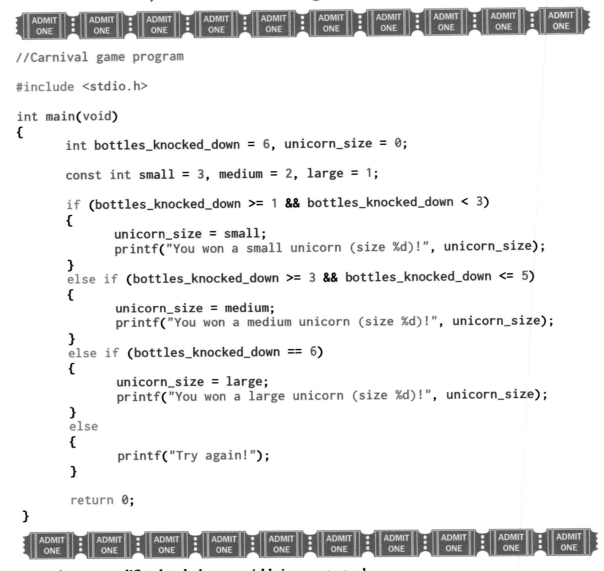

```
//Carnival game program

#include <stdio.h>

int main(void)
{
        int bottles_knocked_down = 6, unicorn_size = 0;

        const int small = 3, medium = 2, large = 1;

        if (bottles_knocked_down >= 1 && bottles_knocked_down < 3)
        {
                unicorn_size = small;
                printf("You won a small unicorn (size %d)!", unicorn_size);
        }
        else if (bottles_knocked_down >= 3 && bottles_knocked_down <= 5)
        {
                unicorn_size = medium;
                printf("You won a medium unicorn (size %d)!", unicorn_size);
        }
        else if (bottles_knocked_down == 6)
        {
                unicorn_size = large;
                printf("You won a large unicorn (size %d)!", unicorn_size);
        }
        else
        {
                printf("Try again!");
        }

        return 0;
}
```

const **is a type qualifier that declares a variable is a constant value:**
const declares that small, medium, and large won't change and can't be modified in the program.

else if **conditions are added to an** if..else **statement to add more test conditions:**
The symbol >= means greater than or equal to and the symbol <= means less than or equal to. If bottles_knocked_down is greater than or equal to 1 AND less than 3, unicorn_size = small. If bottles_knocked_down is greater than or equal to 3 AND less than or equal to 5, unicorn_size = medium. If bottles_knocked_down is equal to 6, unicorn_size = large. Otherwise, the else code block executes. Since bottles_knocked_down has a value of 6, unicorn_size is assigned a large value. The printf() function prints You won a large unicorn (size 1)! on the screen.

We're biking home to: 1 Maple Lane, Sunnyvale, Florida 32004.

```c
//Biking home program

#include <stdio.h>
#include <string.h>

int main(void)
{
        struct Address {
        int street_number;
        char street[100];
        char city[50];
        char state[14];
        int zip_code;
        };

        struct Address home;
        home.street_number = 1;
        strcpy(home.street,"Maple Lane");
        strcpy(home.city,"Sunnyvale");
        strcpy(home.state,"Florida");
        home.zip_code = 32004;

        printf("Bike home to: %d %s, %s, %s %d.", home.street_number, home.street,
        home.city,home.state,home.zip_code);

        return 0;
}
```

The `struct` **statement defines a structure, which is a custom data type that groups variables together:**
It allows you to create a collection of related information. The structure definition in this program contains `int` and `char` variable types. `char` declares a variable with a character data type, which can store a character such as a letter. `Address` is the name that was given to this particular structure type.

A structure's data fields are called members:
This structure contains members `street_number`, `street`, `city`, `state`, and `zip_code`. Each `char` array is an array of characters that allows it to store words as a **string**. Each array length (such as `100` characters for `street`) was chosen to have enough space for the word length.

`home` is declared as an `Address` structure variable:
The `int` members of `home` are accessed and assigned values with the dot (.) operator. The `char` members of `home` cannot be assigned values in this way with the dot operator. `strcpy()` is the string copy function, which is in the C standard library and requires the header file `string.h` to be included. `strcpy()` copies the string `"Maple Lane"` into the `street` member of the `home` structure variable, `"Sunnyvale"` into the `city` member of `home`, and `"Florida"` into the `state` member of `home`.

`%s` in `printf()` is the string format specifier:
`printf()` prints `Bike home to: 1 Maple Lane, Sunnyvale, Florida 32004.` on the screen.

18

We're ordering pizza! If we're very hungry, we'll order 6 cheese pizzas. Otherwise, we'll order one cheese pizza. Since we're very hungry, we're ordering 6 cheese pizzas. Each pizza is $9.99, so the cost of 6 pizzas is 6 x $9.99 = $59.94. The total cost including the delivery cost is $59.94 + $2.99 = $62.93.

```c
//Pizza ordering program

#include <stdio.h>

#define PIZZA_COST 9.99
#define DELIVERY_COST 2.99

int main(void)
{
        int very_hungry = 1, pizza_quantity = 6;
        float total_cost;

        if (very_hungry)
        {
                printf("We're ordering %d cheese pizzas.\n", pizza_quantity);
                total_cost = PIZZA_COST * pizza_quantity;
        }
        else
        {
                printf("We're ordering one cheese pizza.\n");
                total_cost = PIZZA_COST;
        }

        //This means the same as total_cost = total_cost + DELIVERY_COST;
        total_cost += DELIVERY_COST;

        printf("The total cost is $%.2f", total_cost);

        return 0;
}
```

The variable `total_cost` is declared with a `float` data type:
This allows `total_cost` to store a floating-point number (a number that has a decimal point).

Since `very_hungry` equals 1, the `if` condition is true:
`printf()` prints `We're ordering 6 cheese pizzas.` on the screen. The `total_cost` value is set equal to `PIZZA_COST` multiplied by the `pizza_quantity` value of 6.

`DELIVERY_COST` is added to `total_cost` using the `+=` addition assignment operator.

`%f` is the format specifier for a floating-point number:
It is written as `%.2f` because the `.2` in front of `f` specifies that the number will be printed to two decimal places. `printf()` prints `The total cost is $62.93.`

We're having a pizza party! We ate 4 pizzas, so there are 2 extra pizzas.

```c
//Pizza party program

#include <stdio.h>

int party(int pizzas_eaten); //function prototype

int main(void)
{
        int extra_pizza = party(4); //Call the party function

        if (extra_pizza > 1)
        {
                printf("There are %d extra pizzas",extra_pizza);
        }
        else if (extra_pizza == 1)
        {
                printf("There is one extra pizza");
        }

        return 0;
}
int party (int pizzas_eaten)
{
        int pizzas_total = 6;
        int pizzas_left = pizzas_total - pizzas_eaten;
        return pizzas_left;
}
```

A user-defined function allows you to organize your code in a block to perform a specific task: It also allows you to easily re-use a block of code. In this program, party() is a user-defined function that calculates how many pizzas are left over given the number of pizzas eaten. In the party() function, pizzas_eaten is subtracted from pizzas_total and the result is stored in pizzas_left. The party() function returns the value of pizzas_left to the main() function and the value is stored in extra_pizza. Since extra_pizza = 2, the printf() function prints There are 2 extra pizzas.

When a function is called in main() with a function call, the program transfers control to the function: The party() function call is party(4). A function call can pass one or more values to a function, which are called the function call's **arguments**. The party() function call has an argument of 4. A function receives the function call's arguments through variables called **formal parameters**. party() has the formal parameter pizzas_eaten with an int data type that receives the argument value of 4. Once the function is called, its code block is executed. A function can output a return value to main(). The party() function returns pizzas_left to main(). The int before party indicates that the return value is an integer. Once the function ends, control is returned back to main() and the program proceeds.

A function needs to be defined or declared before it is called:
A **function prototype** is a function declaration that allows you to call a function defined after main().

We're at the arcade! If the game choice is 1, we'll play the racing game. If the game choice is 2, we'll play air hockey. If the game choice is 3, we'll play skeeball. If the game choice is 4, we'll play pinball. For all other game choice values, we'll play any other arcade game. Our game choice is 2, so we're playing air hockey.

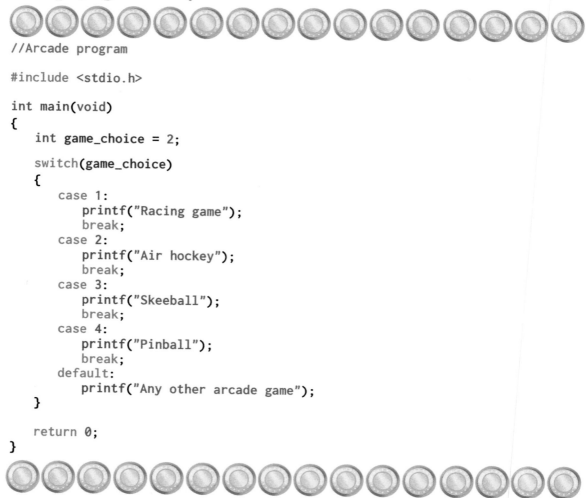

```c
//Arcade program

#include <stdio.h>

int main(void)
{
    int game_choice = 2;

    switch(game_choice)
    {
        case 1:
            printf("Racing game");
            break;
        case 2:
            printf("Air hockey");
            break;
        case 3:
            printf("Skeeball");
            break;
        case 4:
            printf("Pinball");
            break;
        default:
            printf("Any other arcade game");
    }

    return 0;
}
```

A `switch` statement tests if a given value matches a value in a list:
The `switch` statement is an alternative to using a long `if…else if…else` statement to test if an integer value or a character is equal to a value in a list. If there is a matched value in the list, one or more statements associated with the matched value are executed.

The value in parentheses after `switch` is tested for a match in a list of `case` values:
If `game_choice` has a value of 1, the statements under `case 1` are executed and `Racing game` is printed. If `game_choice` has a value of 2, `Air hockey` is printed. If `game_choice` has a value of 3, `Skeeball` is printed. If `game_choice` has a value of 4, `Pinball` is printed. Otherwise, the `default` case is executed and `Any other arcade game` is printed. When a `break` statement is reached, the `switch` statement is exited. Since `game_choice` has a value of 2, `Air hockey` is printed and `break` exits the `switch` statement.

We're bowling! The game has 10 frames and each player gets 2 chances per frame to roll the ball to knock down all the pins. There are 4 of us.

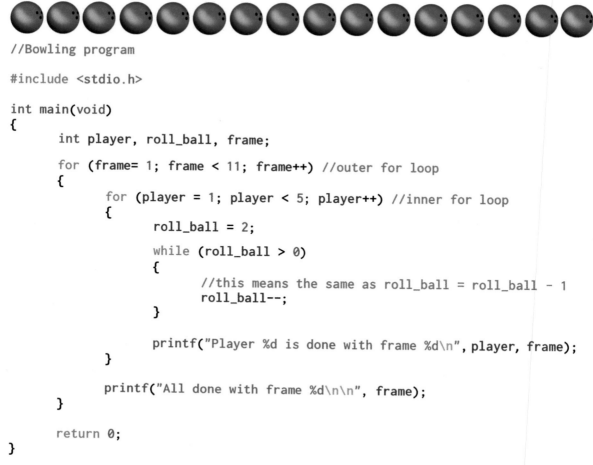

```c
//Bowling program

#include <stdio.h>

int main(void)
{
      int player, roll_ball, frame;

      for (frame= 1; frame < 11; frame++) //outer for loop
      {
            for (player = 1; player < 5; player++) //inner for loop
            {
                  roll_ball = 2;

                  while (roll_ball > 0)
                  {
                        //this means the same as roll_ball = roll_ball - 1
                        roll_ball--;
                  }

                  printf("Player %d is done with frame %d\n", player, frame);
            }

            printf("All done with frame %d\n\n", frame);
      }

      return 0;
}
```

The inner for **loop is called a nested** for **loop:**
The nested for loop is executed during each of the ten iterations of the outer for loop from frame = 1 through frame = 10. The nested for loop has four iterations from player = 1 through player = 4. printf() prints All done with frame 1 at the end of the first iteration of the outer for loop. Two newlines \n\n create an empty line to separate frame numbers. At the end of the last iteration of the outer for loop, printf() prints All done with frame 10.

There is a while **loop inside the nested** for **loop:**
A while loop repeats its code block if the expression in parentheses is still true after each iteration of the loop. In this program, the **decrement operator** -- decreases the value of roll_ball by 1. Since roll_ball begins with a value of 2 and the while expression is roll_ball > 0, the while loop repeats two times. printf() prints the player number and frame number after the while loop ends.

We're in the backyard at night! Since it's not cloudy, we're stargazing for ten minutes and then we'll go back into the house.

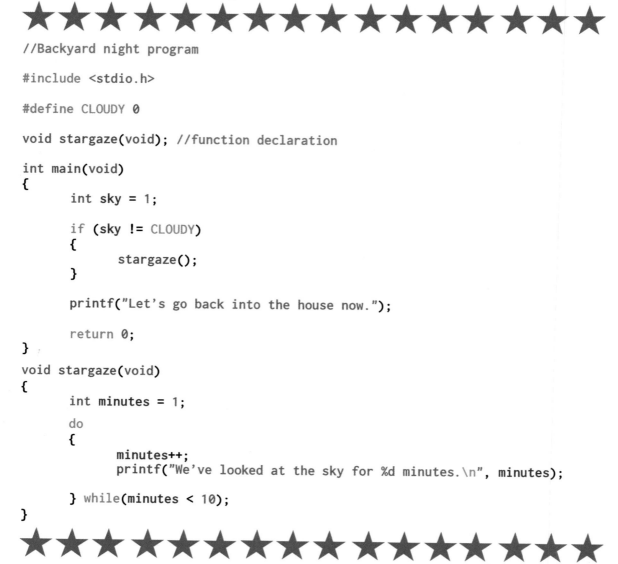

```c
//Backyard night program

#include <stdio.h>

#define CLOUDY 0

void stargaze(void); //function declaration

int main(void)
{
        int sky = 1;

        if (sky != CLOUDY)
        {
                stargaze();
        }

        printf("Let's go back into the house now.");

        return 0;
}
void stargaze(void)
{
        int minutes = 1;
        do
        {
                minutes++;
                printf("We've looked at the sky for %d minutes.\n", minutes);

        } while(minutes < 10);
}
```

The stargaze() function does not have any formal parameters and does not return a value:
Therefore, the function's return type is void and the formal parameter list is void. The purpose of the stargaze() function is to have a separate code block that performs a specific task, which makes the code in main() cleaner and easier to follow. The != operator means "not equal to". Since sky is not equal to CLOUDY, the stargaze() function is called.

The do...while loop in the stargaze() function is a little different than a while loop:
Unlike a while loop, a do...while loop executes once before the while condition is tested. If the while condition is true, the loop will execute again and continue repeating until the while condition is false. Since minutes began at 1 and the while expression is minutes < 10, the loop executes 9 times. The do...while loop prints We've looked at the sky for 10 minutes. at the end of the last loop. The printf() function in main() then prints Let's go back into the house now.

We chose a good movie to watch and made popcorn.

```c
//Movie night program

#include <stdio.h>

int main(void)
{
        char movie_name[100];
        int minutes;

        printf("What movie do you want to watch?\n");

        /* Read a string input from the keyboard (stdin is standard input)
        using the fgets() function that is in the C Standard Library */
        fgets(movie_name,100,stdin);
        printf("Ok, let's watch %s", movie_name);

        printf("How many minutes does it take to make popcorn?\n");
        scanf("%d", &minutes);
        printf("Let's start the movie in %d minutes.\n", minutes);

        char movie_message[] = "Enjoy the show!";
        printf("%s", movie_message);

        return 0;
}
```

A multi-line comment allows you to write a comment over as many lines as you want:
It is created between a forward slash and asterisk /* and an asterisk and forward slash */.

fgets() reads a string input from the keyboard through stdin, which means "standard input":
The character array movie_name is defined with 100 characters to hold enough space for a movie name that will be read into it. The maximum number of characters to be read and stored into movie_name is specified as 100 in fgets(). After you type the movie name and press Enter on the keyboard, the string input is stored in movie_name with a newline character \n and a null character \0 (indicating the end of the string) automatically added to the end of the string. The next printf() function prints the movie_name string in a sentence.

The scanf() function reads an integer input into minutes with the %d format specifier:
After you type the number of minutes and press Enter on the keyboard, the integer input is stored in minutes. The ampersand & operator is used in &minutes because the & operator is required before a variable in scanf() that is not a string. scanf() can only read and store a string if it contains no white spaces, which is why fgets() was used to read in the movie name. The next printf() prints the minutes value read by the scanf() function.

A character array movie_message is declared and initialized as a string in double quotes:
The null character \0 is automatically added to the end of the string to terminate it. The character array size does not need to be included in brackets [] because of the string initialization. The string Enjoy the show! is printed by printf().

We did 10 activities and we're very happy. What an epic day! Goodnight!

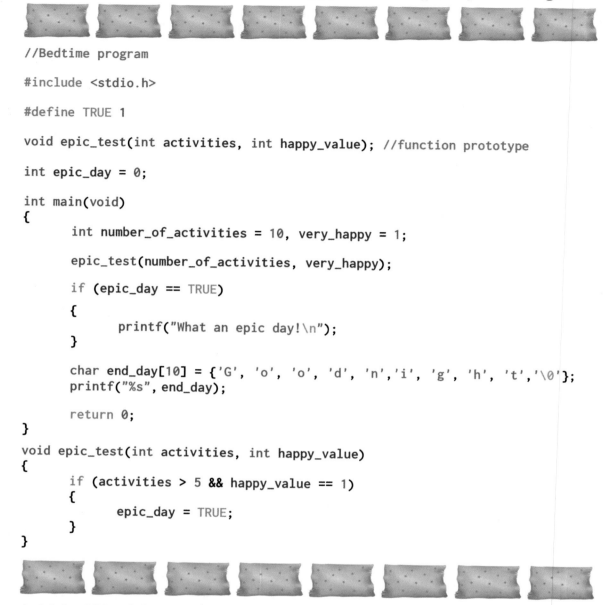

```c
//Bedtime program

#include <stdio.h>

#define TRUE 1

void epic_test(int activities, int happy_value); //function prototype

int epic_day = 0;

int main(void)
{
        int number_of_activities = 10, very_happy = 1;

        epic_test(number_of_activities, very_happy);

        if (epic_day == TRUE)
        {
                printf("What an epic day!\n");
        }

        char end_day[10] = {'G', 'o', 'o', 'd', 'n','i', 'g', 'h', 't','\0'};
        printf("%s", end_day);

        return 0;
}
void epic_test(int activities, int happy_value)
{
        if (activities > 5 && happy_value == 1)
        {
                epic_day = TRUE;
        }
}
```

A global variable is defined outside of any function and can be used by any function in a program:
epic_day is a global variable that can be used by main() and epic_test(). A local variable is defined inside a function and can only be used by that function. A function's formal parameter is a local variable that can have a different name than the function call's argument whose value is copied and passed to it.

Executing the epic_test() function:
number_of_activities and very_happy are arguments in the epic_test() function call. The epic_test() function has two formal parameters, activities and happy_value. Since activities is 10 and happy_value is 1, the epic_day value is set to TRUE. In main(), What an epic day! is printed.

The character array end_day is initialized as the string Goodnight with each letter as an array element:
The array elements are initialized with comma-separated values. The null character \0 must be included to indicate the end of the string because it's not automatically added. The string Goodnight is printed.

Run the programs!

Now you can share the story with YOUR computer! You can run the programs on your computer using a **C compiler,** which converts your **source code** (the code you wrote) into **machine code** that the computer can execute. There are many free C compilers available online. If you search for "free online C compiler", you'll find compilers that run online without requiring a download. This is the link to a good online C compiler called Online GDB:

https://www.onlinegdb.com/online_c_compiler

Type the code in the editor and click the green Run button at the top. You'll see the output of the `printf()` functions in the console at the bottom. If there's an error in your code (such as a missing semicolon or curly brace), you'll see an error message- correct the code and run it again! Change values in the programs (order 20 pizzas instead of 6) and see how the outputs change.

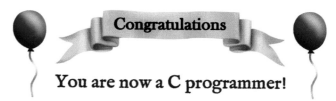

Congratulations

You are now a C programmer!

How can you use C programming?

The C language is widely used in many areas including computer games, graphics, desktop applications, operating systems, databases, and embedded systems. C is the most popular language in embedded systems! An embedded system is a hardware and software system designed to perform one or more specific tasks within a larger system. A **microcontroller** is a common type of embedded system that is in devices and appliances all around you, like your phone, printer, microwave, washing machine, and remote control- just to name a few!

A microcontroller has all the components of a computer contained in a single chip (integrated circuit or **IC**). Just like your computer reads input from the keyboard and outputs text to the screen, a microcontroller reads **inputs** (such as from a sensor or button) and controls **outputs** (such as turning on an LED or motor).

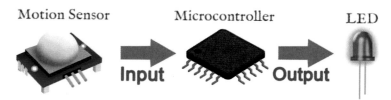

Motion Sensor   Microcontroller   LED

Input   Output

You can apply the syntax and constructs you learned in this book to programming micro-controllers, so you can create your own devices. The Arduino® is a popular microcontroller development platform. The Arduino language is a set of C/C++ functions that you call from your code. For more information about the Arduino platform, please visit: https://www.arduino.cc

Arduino® is a trademark of Arduino SA

Made in the USA
Columbia, SC
29 November 2020